Cambridge **C1 Advanced**

C1 Key Word Transformation

200 exam-styled practice exercises

Jane Turner

www.prosperityeducation.net

Registered offices: Sherlock Close, Cambridge
CB3 0HP, United Kingdom

© Prosperity Education Ltd. 2022

First published 2022

ISBN: 978-1-913825-72-0

This publication is in copyright. Subject to statutory exception
and to the provisions of relevant collective licensing agreements,
no reproduction of any part may take place without the written
permission of Prosperity Education.

'Use of English', 'Cambridge C1 Advanced' and 'CAE' are brands
belonging to The Chancellor, Masters and Scholars of the
University of Cambridge and are not associated with
Prosperity Education or its products.

The moral rights of the author have been asserted.

For further information and resources, visit:
www.prosperityeducation.net

To infinity and beyond

Contents

Introduction	iv
Test 1	1
Test 2	5
Test 3	9
Test 4	13
Test 5	17
Test 6	21
Test 7	25
Test 8	29
Test 9	33
Test 10	37
Test 11	41
Test 12	45
Test 13	49
Test 14	53
Test 15	57
Test 16	61
Test 17	65
Test 18	69
Test 19	73
Test 20	77
Answers	81

Introduction

Welcome to this edition of sample tests for the Cambridge C1 Advanced, Part 4: Key Word Transformation, designed specifically for students preparing for the challenging Use of English section of the (CAE) examination, but also suitable for any English language student working at CEFR C1 level.

C1 results are given against the *Cambridge English Scale*, which is the average score for the four skills and the Use of English section of the test. In order to allow ample time for the reading parts (Parts 5–7) of Paper 1, it is advisable that candidates complete The Use of English section (Parts 1–4) as quickly as possible while maintaining accuracy.

This resource contains 200 exam-styled, single-sentence assessments, each carrying a lexical/lexico-grammatical focus, testing lexis, grammar and vocabulary. Each assessment comprises a sentence, followed by a 'key' word and an alternative sentence conveying the same meaning as the first but with a gap in the middle. Use the key word provided to complete the second sentence so that it has a similar meaning to the first sentence. You cannot change the keyword provided. Each correct answer is broken down into two marks. Next to each sentence transformation answer you will find a guide indicating the focus of the two parts of the answer: either G (grammatical) or L (lexical). At this level, grammar and lexis are often integrated but this device gives a rough indication to help you with your revision for the exam.

Author **Jane Turner** is an associate lecturer in EAP/EFL at Anglia Ruskin University, Cambridge, and an EFL materials writer for international exam boards, universities and publishers. She previously worked as a Cambridge ESOL examiner for the British Council, and holds an MA in Educational Management and Cambridge CELTA and DELTA.

Visit www.prosperityeducation.net for more C1 Advanced exam practice.

Prosperity Education Ltd.
Cambridge, CB3 0HP
United Kingdom

Dear Customer,

Thank you for buying from us.

As an independent publisher, we would really appreciate it if you would leave us your honest feedback.

If you like our resources and what we do, please help us get our story out there.

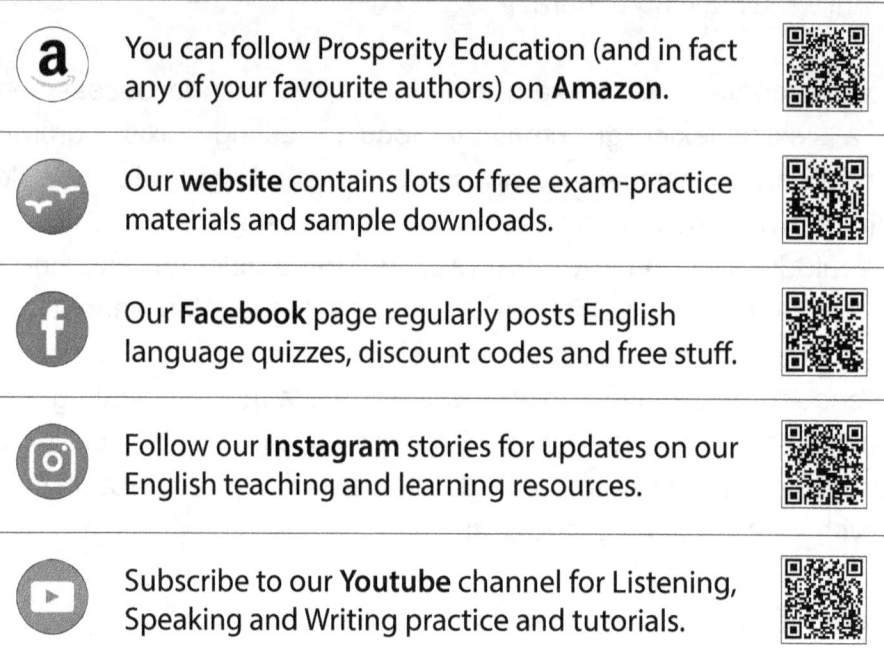

I wish you all the very best for your studies.

Tom O'Reilly, Founder of Prosperity Education

PS. This resource is also available as **a PDF download** from www.prosperityeducation.net Enter the code 10PERCENTPDF at checkout for 10% off.

Cambridge C1 Advanced

Use of English

Part 4

Test 1

Cambridge C1 Advanced Use of English
Part 4 — Key word transformation — Test 1

For questions 1–10, complete the second sentence, using the word given, so that it has a similar meaning to the first sentence. Do not change the word provided and use between three and six words in total. In the separate answer sheet, write your answers in capital letters, using one box per letter.

1 Unfortunately, Luca had to go home immediately after our arrival at the party.

   SOONER

   No _____ Luca had to leave the party.

2 Paul mainly applied to learn more about how the recruitment process works.

   MOTIVATION

   Paul's main _____ learning more about the job market.

3 It was wrong of Marko to assume that I couldn't do the job because of my young age.

   MADE

   Marko _____ my abilities based on my age.

4 After listening to Sofia's suggestions, I'm reconsidering the trip to New York.

   GOT

   Sofia's advice _____ my holiday plans.

5 Even if you have worked before, you will still have to complete initial training.

   REGARDLESS

   You will receive full training _____ previous work experience.

6 My new job gives me not only a rewarding career, but also more free time.

   WORLDS

   I now have _____ in terms of work and leisure.

7 Surely many people opposed the proposal when the council announced it.

   COME

   The council must _____ opposition to the proposal.

8 Being able to analyse information is Lucy's key strength as an employee.

   SKILLS

   Lucy's _____ what makes her so good at her job.

9 I don't think Angelo made the mistake with the order because he was on holiday then.

   BLAME

   Angelo can't _____ for the wrong order.

10 I think the school should stop allowing children to bring mobile phones into class.

   SEE

   I would like to _____ mobile phones from lessons altogether.

Answer sheet: Key word transformation Test No. [ ]

Name _____ **Date** _____

Write your answers in capital letters, using one box per letter.

1.
2.
3.
4.
5.
6.
7.
8.
9.
10.

Cambridge C1 Advanced
Use of English

Part 4

Test 2

Cambridge C1 Advanced Use of English
Part 4 — Key word transformation — Test 2

For questions 1–10, complete the second sentence, using the word given, so that it has a similar meaning to the first sentence. Do not change the word provided and use between three and six words in total. In the separate answer sheet, write your answers in capital letters, using one box per letter.

1. I didn't realise that the number of graduates able to enter their chosen career was so low.

   HOW

   I was surprised to learn _____ in finding employment in their chosen field.

2. It's so annoying that Sue isn't willing to take responsibility for her mistakes.

   ADMIT

   I find Sue's _____ her mistakes very annoying.

3. The band is well worth going to see before they become mainstream.

   DEFINITELY

   You should _____ out before they get too popular.

4. A typical weekday morning for Mateo involves working in his studio.

   WILL

   On weekday mornings, Mateo _____ in his studio.

5 Valentina had not expected to receive an award nomination.

WAS

Being _____ more than Valentina had expected.

6 The problem with arts courses is that they don't receive sufficient funding.

BEING

It seems to me that arts courses _____ properly.

7 Our estimates point to a dramatic increase in the number of people out of work next year.

SET

Unemployment _____ next year.

8 The producers created the series with children under six in mind.

MEANT

The series _____ young viewers originally.

9 Walking there is probably the best option because the bus is so slow.

WELL

Since the bus isn't any faster, we may _____ foot.

10 Despite all my efforts, I wasn't successful.

ABILITY

I did it _____, but I was still unsuccessful.

Answer sheet: Key word transformation Test No.

Name _____ **Date** _____

Write your answers in capital letters, using one box per letter.

1.
2.
3.
4.
5.
6.
7.
8.
9.
10.

Cambridge C1 Advanced
Use of English

Part 4

Test 3

Cambridge C1 Advanced Use of English
Part 4 — Key word transformation — Test 3

For questions 1–10, complete the second sentence, using the word given, so that it has a similar meaning to the first sentence. Do not change the word provided and use between three and six words in total. In the separate answer sheet, write your answers in capital letters, using one box per letter.

1 The only reason I passed was because Pete helped me so much.

   BUT

   I wouldn't _____ all the support Pete gave me.

2 Our customers showed no interest in the vegan food trend.

   CATCH

   Vegan food _____ customers at our restaurant.

3 There is a chance that Jack might do the role temporarily.

   TAKING

   I think Jack _____ the role for a while.

4 Zoe is likely to give the impression of not caring about the problem.

   WELL

   Zoe _____ across as being unsympathetic.

5 Please give me regular updates about the projects you are working on.

POSTED

I'd like you _____ your work projects.

6 Mary's late arrival was the thing that started the argument.

AVOIDED

The argument _____ Mary had arrived on time.

7 I don't understand why Rob chooses to ignore his assistant's rude behaviour.

EYE

Rob should not _____ how rudely his assistant behaves.

8 Because of factors nobody could have expected, the concert had to be cancelled.

DUE

The concert's _____ unforeseen circumstances.

9 Julie impressed everyone by leading the team so well at the training event.

IMPRESSIVE

Julie showed _____ at the training event.

10 I just can't imagine the wallet being stolen by Diego.

HIGHLY

I think it is _____ the wallet.

Answer sheet: Key word transformation   **Test No.**

Name _____   **Date** _____

Write your answers in capital letters, using one box per letter.

1.

2.

3.

4.

5.

6.

7.

8.

9.

10.

Cambridge C1 Advanced Use of English

Part 4

Test 4

Cambridge C1 Advanced Use of English
Part 4 — Key word transformation — **Test 4**

For questions 1–10, complete the second sentence, using the word given, so that it has a similar meaning to the first sentence. Do not change the word provided and use between three and six words in total. In the separate answer sheet, write your answers in capital letters, using one box per letter.

1 There does not seem to be much evidence that the economy is recovering.

ECONOMIC

There are few _____ at the moment.

2 Up to now, Mary has not reached a decision about when she will retire.

UNDECIDED

Mary is as _____ plans.

3 I regret immediately accusing her of lying because it caused us to fall out.

TWICE

Had I _____ accusations about her, we might have stayed friends.

4 Mark's colleagues were irritated because he could never understand their views.

LACK

It was Mark's _____ his colleagues.

5 I had to do my degree all over again when I moved to Sweden.

SCRATCH

Moving to Sweden meant _____ in terms of my studies.

6 The aim of the welcome party is to encourage the students to mix.

TALKING

Hopefully, the party _____ with each other.

7 A partial cause of our falling sales was the rise in inflation.

BLAME

Rising inflation _____ our decreasing sales.

8 If you're not careful, you will be misled by his claims in the interview.

LET

Make sure that you don't _____ during the interview.

9 Sam seems to be completely unconcerned about staying healthy.

WHATSOEVER

Sam has _____ his health.

10 I'm very disappointed that you didn't even suggest my idea at the meeting.

FORWARD

You _____ the idea I told you about.

Answer sheet: Key word transformation Test No.

Name _____ **Date** _____

Write your answers in capital letters, using one box per letter.

1.

2.

3.

4.

5.

6.

7.

8.

9.

10.

Cambridge C1 Advanced Use of English

Part 4

Test 5

Cambridge C1 Advanced Use of English
Part 4 — Key word transformation — Test 5

For questions 1–10, complete the second sentence, using the word given, so that it has a similar meaning to the first sentence. Do not change the word provided and use between three and six words in total. In the separate answer sheet, write your answers in capital letters, using one box per letter.

1 The presentation was a highlight because it was both informative and entertaining.

   DID

   Not _____, but it also kept the audience entertained.

2 In a typical week, the distance she walks is the same as two marathons.

   EQUIVALENT

   She _____ two marathons a week.

3 Not falling off the horse was hard enough to manage, so riding was out of the question.

   ALONE

   I could barely stay on the horse, _____ it.

4 It was a new experience to eat dinner so late at night.

   ACCUSTOMED

   What I was _____ my main meal so late.

5 Maybe Isabel felt that my comments were directed at her when they weren't.

PERSONALLY

Isabel may _____, but that wasn't my intention.

6 It is unclear whether the decision will be in any way significant for the economy.

ECONOMIC

The _____ remains to be seen.

7 Rob definitely seemed like he had a lot of knowledge when I first met him.

ACROSS

Rob did _____ knowledgeable at first.

8 The distinction between being confident and arrogant is not always clear.

LINE

There can be a very _____ confidence and arrogance.

9 Official permission from a teacher is needed for any student taking part in the competition.

CONSENT

Students may not enter the competition _____ their teacher.

10 The architect has not altered the original building design at all yet.

MADE

So far, the architect _____ to the design of the building.

Answer sheet: Key word transformation　　　　　　**Test No.**

Name _____　　**Date** _____

Write your answers in capital letters, using one box per letter.

1.

2.

3.

4.

5.

6.

7.

8.

9.

10.

Cambridge C1 Advanced

Use of English

Part 4

Test 6

Cambridge C1 Advanced Use of English
Part 4 — Key word transformation — **Test 6**

For questions 1–10, complete the second sentence, using the word given, so that it has a similar meaning to the first sentence. Do not change the word provided and use between three and six words in total. In the separate answer sheet, write your answers in capital letters, using one box per letter.

1 It is wrong for schools to give less priority to arts subjects so that they can focus on science.

   PROMOTION

   I do not support _____ the arts in schools.

2 Edward's sense of dedication concerning his research is to be admired.

   HIMSELF

   I admire the way Edward _____ academic career.

3 I expect that it's common knowledge by now that Lucy has resigned.

   HEARD

   You _____ Lucy's departure from the company, I'm sure.

4 The majority of staff employed by the college do not have formal teaching qualifications.

   WHOM

   The college employs many staff, _____ to teach.

5 She reassured me by admitting that she was also feeling nervous.

KNOW

I found _____ she also suffered from nerves.

6 We are sorry that the delay to the train may have been inconvenient.

CAUSED

We would like to apologise _____ the late arrival of the train.

7 There is a strong argument for imposing taxes on sugary food products.

CAN

It _____ taxing foods high in sugar is sensible.

8 We welcome customers suggesting ways in which our service can be improved.

OPEN

We are certainly _____ for improving our service.

9 Perhaps Joe didn't come because he was worried about the cost of the event.

QUESTION

Joe's absence may _____ financial considerations.

10 David will not progress in his career unless he learns to compromise.

REFUSAL

David's _____ him back in work situations.

Answer sheet: Key word transformation   **Test No.**

Name _____ **Date** _____

Write your answers in capital letters, using one box per letter.

1.
2.
3.
4.
5.
6.
7.
8.
9.
10.

Cambridge C1 Advanced

Use of English

Part 4

Test 7

Cambridge C1 Advanced Use of English
Part 4 — Key word transformation — Test 7

For questions 1–10, complete the second sentence, using the word given, so that it has a similar meaning to the first sentence. Do not change the word provided and use between three and six words in total. In the separate answer sheet, write your answers in capital letters, using one box per letter.

1 The best thing about the film was how funny it was.

   ABSOLUTELY

   The film _____, which I liked a lot.

2 If they want to run around and enjoy themselves outside, don't stop them.

   MESS

   Just relax and _____ in the garden.

3 I don't find arguments about the benefits of tax rises convincing.

   THAT

   I am _____ can be particularly beneficial.

4 I have no doubt that the teenage market will respond well to the idea.

   CATCH

   The idea is _____ with teenage consumers.

5 Gary wasn't the world's best dancer, but he was a fantastic singer.

MUCH

Gary may _____ a dancer, but he sang beautifully.

6 Advisors are available to help you should you need it.

HAND

There are _____ can provide assistance.

7 I was very surprised by how much support the team gave me.

BE

I found the team _____, which was very surprising.

8 He was extremely angry about the way the media had covered the event.

OUTRAGED

The media's _____ him.

9 We will save all your files before installing the new software.

PRIOR

Your files will be backed _____ of the new software.

10 We didn't spend too much because Jen monitored our costs carefully.

TRACK

If Jen _____ all our expenses, we might have overspent.

Answer sheet: Key word transformation   **Test No.** ☐

Name _____   **Date** _____

Write your answers in capital letters, using one box per letter.

1.
2.
3.
4.
5.
6.
7.
8.
9.
10.

Cambridge C1 Advanced Use of English

Part 4

Test 8

Cambridge C1 Advanced Use of English
Part 4 — Key word transformation — **Test 8**

For questions 1–10, complete the second sentence, using the word given, so that it has a similar meaning to the first sentence. Do not change the word provided and use between three and six words in total. In the separate answer sheet, write your answers in capital letters, using one box per letter.

1 The potential damage he could do did not bother him at all.

LESS

He _____ about the harm his actions would cause.

2 Due to the non-payment of monthly fees, we have cancelled your membership.

GROUNDS

Your membership has been cancelled _____ you have not paid your fees.

3 The fans hadn't expected the team to do so well this season.

EXCEEDED

The team's performance _____ so far.

4 'Zoe, you really mustn't abandon your ambitions,' said Stefan.

URGED

Stefan _____ up on her dreams.

5 I do not appreciate the loud and angry way in which Jon speaks to the children.

VOICE

I wish Jon _____ at the children.

6 People are finding it virtually impossible to cover their living costs.

ENDS

It is getting _____ each month.

7 Fortunately, the restaurant bill came to far less than expected.

NEARLY

The meal was _____ I had feared.

8 Contacting Monica directly might be worth trying.

HARM

I cannot see there _____ in touch with Monica directly.

9 Doing the housework yesterday meant that I could relax and enjoy my day off.

AS

I cleaned the house yesterday so _____ waste my day off.

10 It is obvious that whoever wrote the review is not a fan of vegetarian cuisine.

HIGH

The reviewer clearly does _____ of vegetarian food.

Answer sheet: Key word transformation Test No. ☐

Name _____ **Date** _____

Write your answers in capital letters, using one box per letter.

1.
2.
3.
4.
5.
6.
7.
8.
9.
10.

Cambridge C1 Advanced
Use of English

Part 4

Test 9

Cambridge C1 Advanced Use of English
Part 4 — Key word transformation — Test 9

For questions 1–10, complete the second sentence, using the word given, so that it has a similar meaning to the first sentence. Do not change the word provided and use between three and six words in total. In the separate answer sheet, write your answers in capital letters, using one box per letter.

1 Students may lose motivation when they are expected to be perfect.

   ABSOLUTE

   Insisting _____ not the best way to motivate students.

2 They are doing nothing to turn what they have learnt into something real.

   PRACTICE

   Their ideas are not _____, for some reason.

3 Eventually, we hope to become the market leaders in menswear.

   ESTABLISH

   The plan is to _____ brand in men's fashion.

4 Trips to galleries and theatres can help students learn more about culture.

   HORIZONS

   Students' _____ by school trips.

5 Votes are being counted by volunteers working night and day.

CLOCK

Teams have been working _____ count the votes.

6 There wasn't a better person to replace Zak than Marcus given the lack of time.

REPLACEMENT

Marcus was the _____ find in the circumstances.

7 The key to guaranteeing good fluency in English is regular study.

ATTAIN

Be consistent with your studying and you _____ of fluency you desire.

8 Since I am weak at public speaking, I asked Lou to give the presentation.

STRONG

Presenting not _____ for me, I asked Lou to do it.

9 Perhaps the website is focused on people thinking of doing a degree.

TARGETING

The website might _____ university students.

10 Despite his demanding job, Jan ensures that he can still take part in family life.

MAKE

Jan always manages _____ his family.

Answer sheet: Key word transformation Test No. ☐

Name _____ **Date** _____

Write your answers in capital letters, using one box per letter.

1.
2.
3.
4.
5.
6.
7.
8.
9.
10.

Cambridge C1 Advanced

Use of English

Part 4

Test 10

Cambridge C1 Advanced Use of English
Part 4 — Key word transformation — Test 10

For questions 1–10, complete the second sentence, using the word given, so that it has a similar meaning to the first sentence. Do not change the word provided and use between three and six words in total. In the separate answer sheet, write your answers in capital letters, using one box per letter.

1 Ali's success shows what you can achieve by trying your hardest.

   MIND

   Ali proves you can succeed if you _____ something.

2 I have never seen Julia look as happy as she does right now.

   EVER

   Julia is _____ before.

3 I suspect that both the online and college course lacked what Geoff needed.

   EITHER

   I do not think that _____ Geoff's needs.

4 Our rental agreement should be renewed shortly.

   FOR

   Our contract is _____ any time now.

5 I am more than happy to give Josh a job recommendation.

HESITATION

I would _____ Josh for the job.

6 We think that you should create a meal plan for the week ahead.

POINT

We would suggest _____ of planning your meals in advance.

7 Why didn't you consult me before taking such an important decision?

OUGHT

I really _____ before you took that decision.

8 We should change our unrealistic expectations of how many people we can hire.

SET

Let's _____ employment targets.

9 It is clear that Alison has the ability to lead and negotiate.

EFFECTIVE

Alison demonstrates not _____ excellent negotiation skills.

10 If you insist on talking throughout the film, you're going to annoy everyone.

NERVES

You are bound _____ if you don't keep quiet during the film.

Answer sheet: Key word transformation Test No.

Name _____ **Date** _____

Write your answers in capital letters, using one box per letter.

1.

2.

3.

4.

5.

6.

7.

8.

9.

10.

Cambridge C1 Advanced
Use of English

Part 4

Test 11

Cambridge C1 Advanced Use of English
Part 4 — Key word transformation — Test 11

For questions 1–10, complete the second sentence, using the word given, so that it has a similar meaning to the first sentence. Do not change the word provided and use between three and six words in total. In the separate answer sheet, write your answers in capital letters, using one box per letter.

1 It was wrong of the school to adhere to such a strict rule in this special case.

   MADE

   I really think the school could _____ given the circumstances.

2 In my opinion, Lou's plan is probably the one that is most likely to work.

   COURSE

   I cannot think of a _____ than Lou's idea.

3 Despite his talents, it is obvious that he is quite insensitive.

   SEEMS

   He may be talented, but he certainly _____ in sensitivity.

4 At some points, I seriously thought that I didn't want to continue the course.

   CLOSE

   There were times when I _____ my degree.

5 Ed never lost his temper despite all the difficulties the project was causing.

HOST

Despite facing _____ problems, Ed remained positive.

6 If we're to be honest, having so much attention from the media distracted us.

FRANKLY

All the media attention _____ from our real work.

7 You'll arrive home after the children's dinner.

WILL

The kids _____ the time you get home.

8 I was not sure about whether I should accept the job offer.

MINDS

I _____ about accepting the job offer.

9 Take plenty of time to decide whether moving abroad is the right decision.

RUSH

Please don't _____ a decision about moving abroad.

10 I didn't offer to help because you didn't update me about your progress.

POSTED

I would have helped you if _____ about any issues.

Answer sheet: Key word transformation Test No.

Name _____ **Date** _____

Write your answers in capital letters, using one box per letter.

1.
2.
3.
4.
5.
6.
7.
8.
9.
10.

Cambridge C1 Advanced
Use of English

Part 4

Test 12

Cambridge C1 Advanced Use of English
Part 4   Key word transformation   Test 12

For questions 1–10, complete the second sentence, using the word given, so that it has a similar meaning to the first sentence. Do not change the word provided and use between three and six words in total. In the separate answer sheet, write your answers in capital letters, using one box per letter.

1 The limited range of vegetarian dishes should be addressed.

   ROOM

   There is _____ terms offering more vegetarian options.

2 Fans couldn't believe that the match was cancelled just twenty minutes before it was due to start.

   SHORT

   Cancelling the match _____ left the fans very frustrated.

3 I was introduced to many people, including some of Maria's oldest friends.

   WHOM

   I met new people at the party, _____ Maria for years.

4 I can't stand the fact that you are so selfish during our holidays.

   ENOUGH

   I have _____ when we go on holiday together.

5 Listening to many different accents is thought to help students' listening skills.

EXPOSURE

Regular _____ may improve listening skills.

6 Lucy was the first person I thought of for the role of team captain.

MIND

Lucy _____ immediately as the person who should be the captain.

7 Focusing on the product that costs the least is not necessarily a smart move.

POSSIBLE

Choosing _____ product might not be wise.

8 We can't expect everything to be how it usually was by the end of the month.

RETURNED

It is unlikely that things _____ by the end of the month.

9 Alessandro possibly did not receive any compensation when his flat was damaged.

BEEN

Alessandro _____ for the damage to his flat.

10 Establishing a business park was the council's choice for the site.

OPTED

The council _____ of a new business park.

Answer sheet: Key word transformation Test No. ☐

Name _____ **Date** _____

Write your answers in capital letters, using one box per letter.

1. ☐☐☐☐☐☐☐☐☐☐☐☐☐
2. ☐☐☐☐☐☐☐☐☐☐☐☐☐
3. ☐☐☐☐☐☐☐☐☐☐☐☐☐
4. ☐☐☐☐☐☐☐☐☐☐☐☐☐
5. ☐☐☐☐☐☐☐☐☐☐☐☐☐
6. ☐☐☐☐☐☐☐☐☐☐☐☐☐
7. ☐☐☐☐☐☐☐☐☐☐☐☐☐
8. ☐☐☐☐☐☐☐☐☐☐☐☐☐
9. ☐☐☐☐☐☐☐☐☐☐☐☐☐
10. ☐☐☐☐☐☐☐☐☐☐☐☐☐

Cambridge C1 Advanced Use of English

Part 4

Test 13

Cambridge C1 Advanced Use of English
Part 4 — Key word transformation — Test 13

For questions 1–10, complete the second sentence, using the word given, so that it has a similar meaning to the first sentence. Do not change the word provided and use between three and six words in total. In the separate answer sheet, write your answers in capital letters, using one box per letter.

1 Julia's original design was far more impressive than what was actually produced.

   ENVISIONED

   What Julia had _____ of an impact than the actual product.

2 Looking at the price of the car she has just bought, I'm assuming that she is rich.

   OR

   She must be rich _____ afforded that car.

3 Nobody manages to reassure people as well as Rob does.

   GIFT

   Rob has a _____ people's minds at ease.

4 We have told them to send everything straight to the venue rather than to our home.

   SENT

   We _____ to the venue directly.

5 There is no question that Zoe gives maximum effort at all times.

THROWS

Zoe certainly _____ whatever she does.

6 Despite falling prices, most people are still unable to afford a house in my town.

MAJORITY

Property remains _____ local people.

7 I did not know what to say when Ruth announced that she was getting married.

SPEECHLESS

Ruth's marriage announcement left _____ shock.

8 There was no justification in the criticism, but I think it motivated me even more.

COMPLETELY

Though the _____, it motivated me to try harder.

9 While everyone was confused at the crime scene, the suspect probably escaped.

AMID

The suspect might _____ at the crime scene.

10 Let's make sure that we know the whole situation before we see the teacher.

GET

We ought _____ straight before talking to the teacher.

Answer sheet: Key word transformation　　　　　　　Test No. ☐

Name _____　　**Date** _____

Write your answers in capital letters, using one box per letter.

1.
2.
3.
4.
5.
6.
7.
8.
9.
10.

Cambridge C1 Advanced
Use of English

Part 4

Test 14

Cambridge C1 Advanced Use of English
Part 4   Key word transformation   **Test 14**

For questions 1–10, complete the second sentence, using the word given, so that it has a similar meaning to the first sentence. Do not change the word provided and use between three and six words in total. In the separate answer sheet, write your answers in capital letters, using one box per letter.

1. All staff and students have the greatest respect for Dr Newman.

    REGARD

    Dr Newman is _____ by staff and students alike.

2. Not a single complaint was made by customers the entire day.

    HEAR

    I did not _____ all during the day.

3. Lack of time was not the reason that Suzie submitted her essay late.

    AMPLE

    Suzie had _____ the essay by the deadline.

4. Many celebrities complain about how fame affects their private life.

    THOSE

    A major problem for _____ eye is lack of privacy.

5 While we expect the best at all times, we still try to support our employees.

SETTING

We try to strike _____ high standards and supporting our staff.

6 Despite the lawyer's best efforts, there was no way the judgment could be disputed.

VAIN

The lawyer searched _____ to appeal the judgement.

7 The event can't take place while the heating is not working properly.

ACTION

Since the heating _____, the event should be postponed.

8 By the end of the year, we hope that the situation will seem more positive.

MAY

Things _____ up by the end of the year.

9 The poor organisation of the festival somewhat affected our enjoyment.

PROPERLY

Had _____, we would have enjoyed it more.

10 'I'm impressed with how much you know about historical subjects,' Zoe said to Peter.

COMPLIMENTED

Zoe _____ of history.

Answer sheet: Key word transformation Test No. ☐

Name _____ **Date** _____

Write your answers in capital letters, using one box per letter.

1. ☐☐☐☐☐☐☐☐☐☐☐☐☐☐
   ☐☐☐☐☐☐☐☐☐☐☐☐☐☐

2. ☐☐☐☐☐☐☐☐☐☐☐☐☐☐
   ☐☐☐☐☐☐☐☐☐☐☐☐☐☐

3. ☐☐☐☐☐☐☐☐☐☐☐☐☐☐
   ☐☐☐☐☐☐☐☐☐☐☐☐☐☐

4. ☐☐☐☐☐☐☐☐☐☐☐☐☐☐
   ☐☐☐☐☐☐☐☐☐☐☐☐☐☐

5. ☐☐☐☐☐☐☐☐☐☐☐☐☐☐
   ☐☐☐☐☐☐☐☐☐☐☐☐☐☐

6. ☐☐☐☐☐☐☐☐☐☐☐☐☐☐
   ☐☐☐☐☐☐☐☐☐☐☐☐☐☐

7. ☐☐☐☐☐☐☐☐☐☐☐☐☐☐
   ☐☐☐☐☐☐☐☐☐☐☐☐☐☐

8. ☐☐☐☐☐☐☐☐☐☐☐☐☐☐
   ☐☐☐☐☐☐☐☐☐☐☐☐☐☐

9. ☐☐☐☐☐☐☐☐☐☐☐☐☐☐
   ☐☐☐☐☐☐☐☐☐☐☐☐☐☐

10. ☐☐☐☐☐☐☐☐☐☐☐☐☐☐
    ☐☐☐☐☐☐☐☐☐☐☐☐☐☐

© 2022 Prosperity Education | 'Cambridge C1 Advanced' and 'CAE' are brands belonging to the Chancellor, Masters and Scholars of the University of Cambridge and are not associated with Prosperity Education or its products.

Cambridge C1 Advanced Use of English

Part 4

Test 15

Cambridge C1 Advanced Use of English
Part 4   Key word transformation   **Test 15**

For questions 1–10, complete the second sentence, using the word given, so that it has a similar meaning to the first sentence. Do not change the word provided and use between three and six words in total. In the separate answer sheet, write your answers in capital letters, using one box per letter.

1   I do not think that the distribution of supplies is reaching the places most in need.

     NOT

     In my opinion, aid _____ to the right places.

2   I think his patience is his best quality as a teacher.

     SUCH

     What _____ teacher is his patience.

3   It was wrong to order stock when you had not asked for permission.

     ORDER

     You should _____ for more stock without permission.

4   If we have to cancel the concert, you will of course receive a full refund.

     FULLY

     Your payments will _____ event of a cancellation.

5 Most people think that the director's time in the army inspired the film.

DRAW

The film is _____ the director's military experiences.

6 She was not chosen despite her test scores being quite high.

RELATIVELY

Though she _____ the test, she was not selected.

7 The prime minister should have clarified the situation during the interview.

RECORD

I wish the prime minister _____ in the interview.

8 After the police were called to the property, the party quickly finished.

END

The party _____ by the police rather rapidly.

9 It must be emphasised that he ensured that all the equipment was tested.

TAKE

Do not forget that he _____ of testing the equipment.

10 Using technological devices is something that Ali finds very easy.

NATURALLY

Learning to use technology seems _____ Ali.

Answer sheet: Key word transformation Test No. ☐

Name _____   **Date** _____

Write your answers in capital letters, using one box per letter.

1. ☐☐☐☐☐☐☐☐☐☐☐☐☐
2. ☐☐☐☐☐☐☐☐☐☐☐☐☐
3. ☐☐☐☐☐☐☐☐☐☐☐☐☐
4. ☐☐☐☐☐☐☐☐☐☐☐☐☐
5. ☐☐☐☐☐☐☐☐☐☐☐☐☐
6. ☐☐☐☐☐☐☐☐☐☐☐☐☐
7. ☐☐☐☐☐☐☐☐☐☐☐☐☐
8. ☐☐☐☐☐☐☐☐☐☐☐☐☐
9. ☐☐☐☐☐☐☐☐☐☐☐☐☐
10. ☐☐☐☐☐☐☐☐☐☐☐☐☐

Cambridge C1 Advanced

Use of English

Part 4

Test 16

Cambridge C1 Advanced Use of English
Part 4 — Key word transformation — **Test 16**

For questions 1–10, complete the second sentence, using the word given, so that it has a similar meaning to the first sentence. Do not change the word provided and use between three and six words in total. In the separate answer sheet, write your answers in capital letters, using one box per letter.

1 Ben's comments should be dismissed as they are probably just gossip.

INCLINED

I would _____ what he said as silly gossip.

2 Jorge didn't listen to the feedback, which is why he was not successful.

BOARD

If Jorge had _____, he might have had more success.

3 If we're focusing on who can be the best leader, Lou is the obvious choice.

COMES

Lou is the best candidate when it _____ a team.

4 It was annoying that this project involved no collaboration whatsoever.

CHANCE

I wish I had had _____ others on this project.

5 Although he had no proof, I believed him as he is usually trustworthy.

WORD

I decided to _____ it because I trust him.

6 I'm sure that the protesters will be in prison long before their lawyers' arrival.

SURELY

The police _____ the protesters by the time the lawyers arrive.

7 Sooner or later, Marek will inevitably have to resign.

MATTER

It is only _____ Marek resigns from his job.

8 I have no idea why Laura dislikes Steve so much.

AGAINST

I am not sure what _____ Steve.

9 We had no authority to alter the document in any way.

AUTHORISED

We were _____ any amendments.

10 I don't fancy going to see the play this evening.

GIVE

I think I will _____ tonight.

Answer sheet: Key word transformation Test No.

Name _____ **Date** _____

Write your answers in capital letters, using one box per letter.

1.
2.
3.
4.
5.
6.
7.
8.
9.
10.

Cambridge C1 Advanced
Use of English

Part 4

Test 17

Cambridge C1 Advanced Use of English
Part 4 — Key word transformation — Test 17

For questions 1–10, complete the second sentence, using the word given, so that it has a similar meaning to the first sentence. Do not change the word provided and use between three and six words in total. In the separate answer sheet, write your answers in capital letters, using one box per letter.

1. We should carry out a lot of renovations to the cottage if we want to sell it.

   OUGHT

   The cottage _____ to attract potential buyers.

2. Student volunteers are welcome to help us organise the concert if they wish.

   ENTIRELY

   Student involvement will be _____ basis.

3. Other audience members were annoyed by Ali talking during the film.

   ANNOYANCE

   Ali kept talking, _____ of the people near him.

4. Tom should include something amusing in the conclusion.

   CONCLUDES

   I suggest that _____ a joke.

5 I would have needed to speak much better Japanese had I accepted the role.

BRUSHING

The job would have meant _____ my Japanese.

6 It is possible that wild horses were not commonly found here.

SIGHT

Wild horses may not _____ in this area.

7 The original design was much better before Ruth made so many amendments to it.

FAR

Ruth has made _____ the original design.

8 We will pay all of your medical bills if surgery is necessary.

UNDERGO

Should _____, we will cover your costs.

9 More than anything else, I could not understand why Paul had stolen the doll.

PUZZLED

What _____ Paul's decision to steal the doll.

10 It would have been easy to make the company's recruitment process better.

EASILY

The company _____ staff more effectively.

Answer sheet: Key word transformation   **Test No.** [ ]

Name _____   **Date** _____

Write your answers in capital letters, using one box per letter.

1.
2.
3.
4.
5.
6.
7.
8.
9.
10.

Cambridge C1 Advanced
Use of English

Part 4

Test 18

Cambridge C1 Advanced Use of English
Part 4 — Key word transformation — Test 18

For questions 1–10, complete the second sentence, using the word given, so that it has a similar meaning to the first sentence. Do not change the word provided and use between three and six words in total. In the separate answer sheet, write your answers in capital letters, using one box per letter.

1 The hotel where we stayed in Paris was an absolute bargain.

   DEAL

   We managed _____ the hotel.

2 Unfortunately, growing my business meant that I had less time for my friends.

   EXPENSE

   I focused a lot on my business, _____ my friendships.

3 I was shocked that the company dismissed Ahmed out of the blue.

   SUDDEN

   I found the company's _____ Ahmed extremely surprising.

4 What made matters even more complicated was the unexpected rail strike.

   FURTHER

   The strike was _____ that we had not expected.

5 Without a doubt, Moira is going to win the tournament this year.

SAFE

I think it _____ will be the new champion.

6 Vito is prepared to do absolutely anything in his quest for fame.

NOTHING

Vito will _____ famous.

7 I don't understand why Anna didn't try her best to find a solution for the customer.

POWER

Anna should have done _____ help the customer.

8 Alan is undeniably an expert in anything related to computer programming.

TALKING

Alan really _____ in terms of programming.

9 Works by that artist tend to sell for approximately $20,000.

REGION

You should expect to _____ $20,000 for a work by that artist.

10 The thing that made Joe stand out from the other candidates was his portfolio.

BASIS

Joe was selected _____ impressive portfolio.

Answer sheet: Key word transformation   **Test No.** ☐

Name _____   **Date** _____

Write your answers in capital letters, using one box per letter.

1
2
3
4
5
6
7
8
9
10

Cambridge C1 Advanced Use of English

Part 4

Test 19

Cambridge C1 Advanced Use of English
Part 4 — Key word transformation — Test 19

For questions 1–10, complete the second sentence, using the word given, so that it has a similar meaning to the first sentence. Do not change the word provided and use between three and six words in total. In the separate answer sheet, write your answers in capital letters, using one box per letter.

1 'I'm not sure if the system that the company has invested in is actually that useful,' said Steve.

   QUESTIONED

   Steve _____ his company's new IT system.

2 Generally speaking, the food we ate while on holiday was excellent.

   PART

   The food while we were away _____, very good.

3 Researchers suspect that this was possibly not the only region that produced the pottery.

   UNIQUE

   This type of pottery may _____ this area.

4 Julie only cares about getting what she wants, whatever the consequences.

   OWN

   As long as Julie _____, she is happy.

5 Growing public dissatisfaction was evident from the large-scale protests.

REFLECTION

The protests were _____ dissatisfied people had become.

6 Accepting new jobs would not be a wise move for me at the moment.

INTERESTS

It is probably _____ any more work right now.

7 There is no point in worrying now about everything that we didn't do very well.

DWELL

Let's _____ have done better.

8 The design shows that the vehicle will be completely solar-powered.

RUN

The vehicle is _____ energy from the Sun.

9 Sue went over everything with me so that I could understand what had been covered.

SPEED

Sue _____ what I had missed during my absence.

10 I made the promise to you because I knew I could fulfil it.

WORD

I would not _____ if I doubted I could do it.

Answer sheet: Key word transformation Test No.

Name _____ **Date** _____

Write your answers in capital letters, using one box per letter.

1.
2.
3.
4.
5.
6.
7.
8.
9.
10.

Cambridge C1 Advanced Use of English

Part 4

Test 20

Cambridge C1 Advanced Use of English
Part 4 — Key word transformation — Test 20

For questions 1–10, complete the second sentence, using the word given, so that it has a similar meaning to the first sentence. Do not change the word provided and use between three and six words in total. In the separate answer sheet, write your answers in capital letters, using one box per letter.

1 It was impossible for the company to expand as quickly as the main competitors.

PACE

There was no way the company _____ its rivals.

2 Everyone expects Ruth to be the person who eventually takes over from Max.

LIKELY

Ruth is the _____ to Max.

3 We should specify what duties the role involves.

PROVIDED

Clear job _____ to show what we expect.

4 Nothing seemed to make the guests happy at any point while they were here.

DURATION

The guests looked miserable _____ their stay.

5 We hope that the new initiative will teach more people how to read and write.

RATES

We hope that _____ rise thanks to the initiative.

6 It is extremely hard to make an accurate prediction about the election winner.

CERTAIN

Saying _____ this election is virtually impossible.

7 The constant lack of sleep left me feeling very confused most of the time.

STRAIGHT

I was _____ anything because I was exhausted.

8 We are developing a new type of tablet that will protect people from the Sun.

FORM

Our latest innovation is sun protection _____ tablet.

9 Joining Mike's team was awkward because I had previously criticised him a lot.

POSITION

Working with Mike _____ as I'd been his main critic.

10 All the negative publicity about him is likely to affect his popularity soon.

PRESS

Unless he _____ soon, he will become unpopular.

Answer sheet: Key word transformation Test No.

Name _____ **Date** _____

Write your answers in capital letters, using one box per letter.

1.

2.

3.

4.

5.

6.

7.

8.

9.

10.

Answers

Answers — Key word transformation — Test 1

#				
1	sooner had we	arrived than	G	L
2	motivation for/behind	applying was	L	G
3	has made	(incorrect) assumptions about / an (incorrect) assumption about	G	L
4	got me	(thinking about) reconsidering/reassessing	G	L
5	regardless	of (any/your)	L	G
6	the best	of both worlds	G	L
7	have come	up against (strong/stiff)	G	L
8	analytical skills	are what	L	G
9	have been	to blame for	G	L
10	see the school	ban	L	G

Answers — Key word transformation — Test 2

#				
1	how few/many graduates	(actually) succeed / are (actually) successful	G	L
2	unwillingness to admit	to	L	G
3	definitely check	them / the/that/this band	L	G
4	will (typically)	be / work / be working / be found working	L	G
5	nominated for	an/the award was	G	L
6	are not being	funded	G	L
7	Looks/is set to	rise/increase/grow (dramatically)	G	L
8	was meant	(to be) for	G	L
9	as well go	(there) on	G	L
10	to the best of	my ability	L	G

Answers — Key word transformation — Test 3

1	have passed	but for	G	L	
2	didn't/did not catch	on with (the)	G	L	
3	may/might/could be	taking (on)	G	L	
4	could/may/might well	come	G	L	
5	to keep me posted	on	L	G	
6	could/would/might have been	avoided if/had	G	L	
7	turn	a blind eye to	G	L	
8	cancellation	was due to	L	G	
9	impressive	leadership (qualities/skills)	G	L	
10	highly unlikely/improbable	(that) Diego stole	L	G	

Answers — Key word transformation — Test 4

1	signs/indications of	economic recovery	G	L	
2	yet undecided about	her retirement	G	L	
3	thought twice	before/about making	L	G	
4	lack of understanding	that irritated	L	G	
5	starting / (that) I had to start	from scratch (again)	G	L	
6	will/can	get (the) students talking	G	L	
7	was partially to	blame for	G	L	
8	let him	mislead you / make misleading claims	G	L	
9	(absolutely) no concern(s)	whatsoever for	L	G	
10	could/should have	put forward	G	L	

Answers — Key word transformation — Test 5

#				
1	only did the presentation / only did it	inform	G	L
2	walks the equivalent	of	G	L
3	let alone	ride	L	G
4	not accustomed to	was eating/having	L	G
5	have taken the/my comments	personally	G	L
6	economic significance	of the decision	L	G
7	come	across as (being)	G	L
8	fine/thin line	between	L	G
9	without	(getting) the consent of	L	G
10	hasn't/has not	made any alterations/changes	G	L

Answers — Key word transformation — Test 6

#				
1	the promotion of science	over	L	G
2	dedicates himself / has dedicated himself	to his	L	G
3	will/must have	heard about	G	L
4	most/many of whom	are unqualified / aren't/are not qualified	G	L
5	it reassuring	to know (that)	L	G
6	for any/the inconvenience	caused by	L	G
7	can be	argued that	G	L
8	open to	customer suggestions / customers' suggestions / any suggestions / suggestions	L	G
9	have been	a question of	G	L
10	refusal/inability	to compromise is holding	G	L

Answers — Key word transformation — Test 7

#				
1	was	absolutely hilarious	G	L
2	let them mess	around/about	G	L
3	not convinced that / unconvinced that	raising taxes / tax rises	L	G
4	going/certain to / certainly going to	catch on	G	L
5	not have been	much of	G	L
6	advisors/people	on hand that/who	L	G
7	to be	(very) supportive	G	L
8	coverage of the event	outraged	L	G
9	up	prior to (the) installation	L	G
10	hadn't/had not kept	track of	G	L

Answers — Key word transformation — Test 8

#				
1	couldn't/could not have	cared less	G	L
2	on	the grounds that	G	L
3	has exceeded	(the) fans' expectations / expectations	G	L
4	urged Zoe not to	give	G	L
5	wouldn't/would not	raise his voice	G	L
6	hard/harder/impossibe to make	ends meet	G	L
7	not nearly	as expensive as	G	L
8	being any	harm in getting	G	L
9	so as	not to	L	G
10	not have / hold	a high opinion	G	L

Answers — Key word transformation — Test 9

#				
1	on	absolute perfection is	G	L
2	being put	into practice	G	L
3	establish ourselves	as the leading / as the top	G	L
4	(cultural) horizons	can be broadened/expanded/widened	L	G
5	around/round the clock / round the clock	to	L	G
6	best replacement	we could	L	G
7	will (certainly)	attain the level/standard	G	L
8	being	a strong point	G	L
9	be targeting	prospective/potential	G	L
10	to make	time for	G	L

Answers — Key word transformation — Test 10

#				
1	put your mind	to	L	G
2	looking	happier than ever	G	L
3	either of the courses / either course	met/fulfilled	G	L
4	due/up for	renewal	G	L
5	have no	hesitation in recommending	G	L
6	(that) you make / making	a point	G	L
7	ought to have been	consulted	G	L
8	set	(more) realistic	G	L
9	only effective leadership	but also	G	L
10	to get on	somebody's/everyone's/people's nerves	G	L

Answers — Key word transformation — Test 11

#				
1	have made	an exception	G	L
2	better	course of action	G	L
3	seems to be	lacking	G	L
4	came/was close to	quitting/abandoning	G	L
5	a (whole) host	of	L	G
6	was frankly	a distraction	G	L
7	will have eaten / will have eaten/had dinner	by	G	L
8	was	in two minds	G	L
9	rush	into making / into coming to / into / to	G	L
10	you had kept	me posted	G	L

Answers — Key word transformation — Test 12

#				
1	room for improvement	in	L	G
2	at	(such) short notice	G	L
3	some of whom	had/have known	L	G
4	had enough of	your selfishness	G	L
5	exposure to	(many) different accents	L	G
6	came/sprang to	mind	G	L
7	the cheapest	possible	G	L
8	will have returned	to normal	G	L
9	might/may not have been	compensated	G	L
10	opted for	the establishment/opening of	L	G

Answers — Key word transformation — Test 13

1	envisioned would have	had more	G	L
2	or	she couldn't/could not have	L	G
3	gift for	putting/setting	G	L
4	are having everything	sent	G	L
5	throws herself/everything	into/at	L	G
6	unaffordable for	the majority of	L	G
7	me speechless	with/due to / out of	L	G
8	criticism was	completely unjustified	G	L
9	have escaped	amid the confusion	G	L
10	to get	our/the facts	G	L

Answers — Key word transformation — Test 14

1	held	in high regard / the highest regard	G	L
2	hear any customer complain/complaints	at	L	G
3	ample time	(in which) to submit	L	G
4	those	in the public	G	L
5	a balance between	setting	L	G
6	in vain for	some way / a way	L	G
7	is	out of action	G	L
8	may	look up / be looking up / pick up / be picking up	G	L
9	the festival been organised	properly	G	L
10	complimented Peter	on his knowledge	G	L

Answers — Key word transformation — Test 15

1	is not being	distributed	G	L
2	makes him	such a good	L	G
3	not have	placed an order	G	L
4	be fully refunded	in the	L	G
5	thought to / believed to	draw on	G	L
6	scored relatively highly / performed/did relatively well	on/in	L	G
7	had set / had put	the record straight	G	L
8	was brought	to an end	G	L
9	did take	the precaution of	G	L
10	to come	naturally to	G	L

Answers — Key word transformation — Test 16

1	be inclined to	dismiss/treat	G	L
2	taken	the feedback on board / on board the feedback	G	L
3	comes to	heading (up)/ leading	G	L
4	a/the chance to	collaborate/work with	G	L
5	take	his word for	G	L
6	will surely have	imprisoned	G	L
7	a matter of time	before	L	G
8	Laura/she has	against	L	G
9	not authorised to	make	G	L
10	give	the play a miss	G	L

Answers — Key word transformation — Test 17

#				
1	ought to be	(fully/completely) renovated / renovated completely/fully	G	L
2	on an	entirely voluntary	G	L
3	much to	the annoyance	G	L
4	Tom/he concludes	with	G	L
5	brushing up	on	L	G
6	have been	a common sight	G	L
7	far too many	modifications to	G	L
8	you need/have to	undergo surgery	G	L
9	puzzled me	(the most) was	L	G
10	could easily have / could have easily	recruited	G	L

Answers — Key word transformation — Test 18

#				
1	to get/find/secure	a great/good/cheap deal on	G	L
2	at the expense	of	L	G
3	sudden dismissal	of	L	G
4	a further	complication	G	L
5	is safe to say/assume	that Moira	L	G
6	stop at nothing	to be/become/get	L	G
7	everything in her power	to	L	G
8	knows what	he's/he is talking about	G	L
9	pay/spend/get	(something/somewhere) in the region of	L	G
10	on the basis	of his	G	L

Answers — Key word transformation — Test 19

1	questioned the (actual) usefulness/value	of	G	L
2	was,	for the most part	G	L
3	not have been	unique to	G	L
4	gets/has	her (own) way	G	L
5	a reflection of	how	L	G
6	not in my (best) interests	to accept	L	G
7	not dwell on/upon	what we should/could	L	G
8	going to / designed to	run (completely/entirely) on	G	L
9	brought me	up to speed with/on	G	L
10	have given you	my word	G	L

Answers — Key word transformation — Test 20

1	could keep	pace with	G	L
2	(most) likely	successor	G	L
3	specifications/descriptions/requirements	should be provided	L	G
4	for the (entire) / throughout the	duration of	L	G
5	literacy rates / rates of literacy	will	L	G
6	for certain	who will win	L	G
7	not thinking	straight about	G	L
8	in	the form of a	G	L
9	put me	in a difficult position	G	L
10	gets/receives/has	(some) good press	L	G

Notes

Notes

Notes

www.ingramcontent.com/pod-product-compliance
Lightning Source LLC
Chambersburg PA
CBHW081918090526
44590CB00019B/3401